THOUGHTS FROM A REASONING MIND

POETRY & MUSINGS

THOUGHTS FROM A REASONING MIND

POETRY & MUSINGS
BY AKILAH MOSELEY

Published by: I.AM.

1st Edition 2008
2nd Edition 2013

Published by: I. AM.

ISBN: 978-0-9927839-0-7

FROM ME..

The work within this book has been a real venture. What started out as a hobby, writing in the comfort of my home, progressed into a challenge to step out of my comfort zone.

It would not be right to call this book a labour of love...however, it has been fun, and in its own way a journey of discovery.

This collection offers a selection of work spanning a two year period. Having produced this book in order to share with family, and then later on in response to a wider poetry audience, I remain amazed at the need to meet demand with the production of this 2nd Edition.

Even more amazing is the fact that this book is now the first of a series of books on offer under the "Thoughts of a Reasoning Mind" umbrella.

I have kept the contents and design true to the original format and as always offer these Thoughts from a Reasoning Mind as my gift ..to you

ENJOY!

Akilah

Akilah

CONTENTS

LONG ROAD

ROOF TO KEEP, BILLS TO PAY
FOOD TO COOK, NO DELAYS

Take a walk with me on the long road

CLOTHES TO WASH, GRASS TO CUT
CAR TO MAINTAIN, STUCK IN A RUT

Take a walk with me on the long road.

NO-ONE TO TALK TO, KIDS MY SOLE COMPANY
MISSED THE OPPORTUNITY, TO BE YOUNG AND
FREE

Take a walk with me on the long road

WORKING HARD FOR THE SALARY
JUST ABOUT COVERING THE NURSERY FEE

Take a walk with me on the long road

LIVING PAYDAY TO PAYDAY, ENDS NEVER MEET
SHOULDERING ASSUMPTIONS OF OTHERS, THAT
EVERYTHING IS SWEET
Take a walk with me on the long road

BIRTHDAYS; CHRISTMAS; EASTER & SUMMER
NEVER SURE WHAT I'LL BE ABLE TO COVER

Take a walk with me on the long road

TEMPTATION TO **SPEND**, NOT EVEN ON ME
NO TREATS OR SURPRISES, WHAT A TRAGEDY

Take a walk with me on the long road

"IT'S BEST TO HAVE THEM TOGETHER"
"DON'T WORRY, THEY'LL SOON BE BIG"
"TWO ARE EASIER THEN ONE"
THE ANECDOTES KEEP GOING ON AND ON

Take a walk with me on the long road

TAPS, WITH NO RUNNING WATER. PLASTER
FALLING OFF THE WALLS
"MUMMY WHEN ARE WE GETTING A NEW
HOUSE?"
ANOTHER T.V LICENSE CALL

Take a walk with me on the long road

TAKES 2 TO MAKE A BABY. ONE TO BE
RESPONSIBLE BY LAW
IT'S GOT TO HAVE BEEN A MAN TO HAVE
CREATED SUCH A FLAW

Take a walk with me on the long road

NO SEMBLANCE OF MY OWN LIFE. AT THE
CHILDREN'S BECK & CALL.
OTHER PEOPLES GUARANTEE, BABY SIT THEIR
CHILDREN, ONE AND ALL

Take a walk with me on the long road

MONOTONY, MUNDANE
BEHIND THE TIMES, LETHARGY

Take a walk with me on the long road

JUST ANOTHER STATISTIC
WORKING TAX CREDIT, GOVERNMENT SUBSIDY.
THIS BRANCH COULDN'T HAVE FALLEN, ANY
FURTHER AWAY FROM THE TREE

Take a walk with me on the long road

WHATS UP AHEAD, A TURN OFF! A SHORT CUT!
T-JUNCTION... OR MAYBE A DEAD END STREET.
PROBABLY A LONG ASS DIVERSION, TAKING THE
MICKEY OUT OFME

Take a walk with me on the long road

FEET TIRED AND ACHING. HEAD IS KILLING ME
BACK BROKEN, TUNNEL VISION
THIS IS THE LIFE FOR ME

Take a walk with me on the long road

Love tastes like the first drop of
Ice placed upon the tongue – Electric
sharp & cool.

Love tastes like the rich creamy
smoothness of chocolate dessert -
too irresistible to decline.

Love tastes like bubble gum,
artificial yet fruity.

14

REFLECTIONS

Do you know what you want? Do you really know?
Or do you only think you want what you see?

Do you realise that what you profess to love in its
entirety and for its nicety is the way that it is and is
no more? There is no reserve tank to expect.

Do you understand that actually, this is no game?
Life and all it throws at you is hard enough, and
sometimes, sometimes, there is nothing to laugh
about.

Can you handle that?

Can you appreciate that actually love cannot conquer
all and, oftentimes it is the smallest thing that swings
the balance... the wrong way.

Are you honest enough to let your actions speak
louder?
To allow yourself to be judged on your deeds and not
on your ability to persuade everyone to take your side,
see your view, to allow you the proverbial "Cake and
eat it too"

Can you foresee longevity of challenge and unrelenting battle?
A definite no retreat and no surrender. Where a fairy tale "ever after" is no guarantee?

Can you?

Look into your eyes.

Can you?

Search inside your heart.

Can you?

Feel the fear reverberate through your soul.

Does this frighten you?

BEAUTY

Beauty is looking at yourself in the mirror
and smiling widely.

Beauty is an inner radiance that cannot
be shut in.

Beauty is the whizz and flash of fireworks,
bright colours against a dark sky

Beauty is being surrounded by those
who love and accept you for you,
no, but maybe....

Beauty is **Being**
         Eternally
         Alive
         Unique
         True
         Inspirational
         Funny
         Ultimately
         Loved.

      Beautiful

HONEY, CAN'T YOU SLEEP?

Honey, can't you sleep? What's wrong? Why aren't you sleeping?

Questions come fast and furious. It is not that she cannot sleep. It is that she has been caught in the gap between consciousness and that other place, where we attempt to let the body, if not the mind rest.

She feels the palm of his hand slide up her thigh and rest on the middle of her stomach, covering her belly, desperate to explore, but yet, but yet not secure in the timing of the movement.

She places her hand over the other already on her stomach,
Covering and interlocking their fingers, She assists the palm to travel across her body, swallowing her in an embrace..."go back to sleep" she replies. "I'm ok, I'll be sleeping soon".

Silence hangs in the air, suspended in motion.
Stillness prevails, no evidence even of breath,
The inhaling and exhalation of each other hover above them but is not visible to either of them.

She feels his hand release from within her own and again travel down her frame. However this time it does not rest above her centre, but continues to slide into the dip of the meeting of her groin and thigh. Fingers splayed, they stroke the opening of her vagina, teasing the labia, in a rhythmic motion.

"Go back to sleep" she murmurs again, halting the fingers, but it is too late. Those fingers and the hand that owns it are now unstoppable.
Erratically and with urgency unexplained they search deeper and deeper within her. The whole hand and its twin, pries open her thighs like a patrolman at the border has granted entry to paradise.

And in that moment she realises...

There will be no more sleep before morning.

VEX!

It's not you. I wish I could just give it away, but I can't. I know it's me.

But knowing that it's me, that I am the cause of all this tension, doesn't help. If anything it just aggravates me more.

Being in your presence should have me grinning from ear to ear. Believe me when I say that I honestly try to lighten my mood. I am struggling to meet you half way.

I have to say it doesn't help that you do not even offer to take on the blame!
Not a "What can I do?" "I accept that I have played a part in this..." "I'm so sorry..."

You just sit, in silence, feeling uncomfortable. Then you just say "bye" and put down the phone or, put on your coat and go home.

I totally understand that this is not of your making, and has nothing to do with you.

But I'm still VEX!

CUNNING GUS

TALL AND ERECT, BROAD AND WIDE
ALERT AND AT THE READY
OPTIC EYE GLISTENING

CUNNING GUS ENTERS THE VOID
INSTANTLY OVERWHELMED
DARKNESS SURROUNDS, WITH HINTS OF WHITE
GLARE
INITIAL FEAR REPLACED WITH A KALEIDOSCOPE,
OF....

WARMTH AND WETNESS, QUICKLY SUPERSEDED
WITH HEAT AND PULSATING RHYTHMS OF
DISTANT FORGOTTEN FLASHBACKS OF
PREVIOUS ESCAPADES, THEN...

RESUMING CONTROL CUNNING GUS PUSHES
ONWARDS
DEFYING GRAVITY.
DEEPER AND DEEPER, YET HIGHER AND HIGHER
THE RUSH OF ENDORPHINS, PRE-EMPTING THE
DISPLAY OF LIGHT AND COLOUR ABOUT TO
COME.

AT THE SUMMIT
ENVELOPED IN THICK MOIST SHOWERS
WEARY AND DRAINED, PRESUMED WASTED

THERE IS THE SLIGHTEST OF MOVEMENT
THE TINIEST TWITCH
AND THEN THE OPTIC EYE ROUSES
A SALUTE TO CUNNING GUS

STEPPING OUT IN FAITH

Every self-help book tells you that you know when things in your life need to change. They testify to the need to "heed the lesson", "get out of the valley" or to "let go".
If we are honest, these are probably the same words of wisdom we have offered to our nearest, dearest, closest friends, siblings and colleagues in their most difficult life challenges. But somehow, it is not so cut and dried when we are the recipients of these same wise words.

When the statement changes from "you need to..." to "I need to..." automatically we see the cup being half full, no longer half empty. We automatically, in the initial stages at least, justify why situations and episodes are not necessarily as black and white as others see. As we begin to pinpoint the kaleidoscope of colour that makes our experience that bit different from the norm, we spiral down that helter skelter of battered emotions and bruised egos.

We know however that the only person we are fooling is ourselves!
We have that tacit knowledge that when all is over and done with, the person who will ultimately have suffered the worst for prolonging that which we know we have to do, will be us.

But we continue to deceive ourselves into thinking that we need to "monitor it" a little longer. "Sleep on it" for a while. Balance the pros and the cons, whilst all the time just avoiding what we know to be unavoidable.

How comforting a zone in which to procrastinate, bury our heads, distract.
Whilst on the inside our bodies begin to bear witness to the dis-ease that befalls us. As we begin to lose/gain weight, fight off infections and colds, become lethargic, depressed and vent our frustrations on others smaller or less powerful than us, we tell others that we "probably need some time out" from the hectic work/life imbalance.

When in fact we know, that it is not time we need. We know that time is long overdue for ACTION.

As with most self help manuals, gurus and griots, it is at this point that you would begin the 10-step plan of action. However, back to being honest. We know that the 10-step plan will never deliver, as we will have read through them and decided:

1. It doesn't suit our situation
2. It's way too difficult to commit to
3. Things aren't really as bad as we thought

However, isn't it strange that it is at this point that those around us begin to mirror the experience we are fighting with?
Conversations in the office touch a nerve with us, books and music we encounter wax lyrical on parallel lines to the situation that we are pretending is non-existent.

This is not a fluke.
This is the universes way of being in your face and reminding you of your responsibility to get your house in order.
To warn you that what is done/kept in the dark will come to light...

Taking ACTION is not about endings or closure.
It is acknowledging that at this point in time, right here right now I am not in a comfortable space, and because I am not comfortable I am being PRO-ACTIVE in creating a much needed shift.
Taking ACTION is the belief that your needs are just as important as the next person's. No more, and definitely no less.

When it is broken down in this clear simple form it is then easier to act in good faith and start a dialogue with those concerned.

We can act in good faith knowing that even if the outcome is not what we would have liked or hoped for... that we did not allow our fear of evaluation and joint decision making to supersede our own value and self-worth, nor strip us of our dignity.

LEST WE FORGET

We are young, we are gifted we are black
Before our enslavement we built empires, communities
and villages. We were scientists, physicians and
astrologers.
LEST WE FORGET

During our enslavement we picked cotton, ploughed
fields, ran households. And, still made time to plan
our freedom.
LEST WE FORGET

Following our freedom we continued to tend the sick,
toil the land and await our forty acres and a mule.
LEST WE FORGET

Generations later as we again came into our own
We invented traffic lights, fought wars, developed
communications and performed the first live open
heart surgery
LEST WE FORGET

In the fifties and sixties we built up the transport
systems, staffed the hospitals fought the punks and
the Mods and initiated Europe's largest carnival
LEST WE FORGET

Today in the 2000's
We are no longer our "brother's keeper"
We no longer build empires
We no longer nurture community
We no longer seek the Promised Land

Who will be there, to lead our children?

LEST THEY FORGET?

ART OF FLIRTATION

It is the glance that locks on another
The 2-second connection that feels like 10
It is the sudden rush of heat to your face

THIS IS THE ART OF FLIRTATION

It is the sudden fingering of your hair
The constant playing with your ears
The repetition of another's phrase

THIS IS THE ART OF FLIRTATION

It is the testing of newfound boundaries
The conversing with suggestive ease
Unconscious acts that tease.

THIS IS THE ART OF FLIRTATION

It is the flurry of emails sent
Nights out after work spent
A quick brush of lips goodnight

THIS IS THE ART OF FLIRTATION

It is daily contact by phone
Popping over to each others homes
No longer comfortable being alone

THIS IS THE ART OF FLIRTATION

It is receiving invitations for 2
Seeing each other in the nude
Beginning to live in each other's shoes

THIS IS THE ART OF FLIRTATION

It is having no time for friends of old
No longer fitting in your old mould
Interactions running both hot & cold.

THIS IS THE ART OF FLIRTATION

It is slowly going round the bend
Refusing to accept the end
Not believing your life will ever mend

THIS IS THE ART OF FLIRTATION

FEELING HORNY

Oestrogen level rising higher
My skins tingling on fire
Hairs on my arms begin to raise
Recognition that I'm entering that phase

Wetness in between my thighs
I slowly begin to close my eyes
Nipples swell and thicken
Heart rate starts to quicken

Breasts now firm and taut
Nerves are getting fraught
Trying to take things slowly
But thinking of me only

Picturing our limbs intertwined
You taking me from behind
Imagining your sweat running down my spine
Not content to view such thoughts in my mind

Eager to call you on the phone
To tell you to hurry and come on home
But, my desires burning strong
Won't be able to hold out long

Fingers delve, now moist and slick
My breathing now erratic, quick
Orgasmic waves cascade and slam
GOD DAMN........

I'm feeling horny!

DEEPEST DESIRE

Looking back visions of laughter, frivolity, oneness,
surround me.
I inhale the fragrance of our first tentative kiss and
the sparks of electricity that flooded my system.

I remember jumping feet first into the headiness of
meeting my kindred spirit, my forever after, my
continuous ascent towards our lifetime.

Basking in the glow of positivity, you challenged me to
think about me.
To allow others to do for me, support me, help me….
And I struggled with this alien concept reassured
that, as ever you were there to hold my hand.

Centered in your warm embrace I became hungry,
rooting like a newborn.
Discovering the magnitude of my abilities. Learning
and accepting my worth and now able to recognise the
opportunities I was once scared to grasp or to claim.

Looking back I have visions. I inhale the fragrance. I
feel sparks.
Deep within my epicentre I desire to become a time
traveller. To hold the power to frequent this time,
this life, this feeling.

But I cannot.

I cannot look back. I am not a time traveller, and I
refuse to become a time traveller's wife.
I have a deeper desire burning within me now.
I am looking forward.

DEDICATION

May I present to you my story
An epic tale full of glory
One that has taken over 3 decades for me to
understand
Come, journey with me as I lay out the land.

Travels far away from her country of birth
One ticket, one suitcase, to share a room with sibling
and friends to make, create a new

Meets a man, dashing, hard working and stable
Together they start out - this is no fable.
They develop a true partnership, through necessity
and responsibility
As where there is love, ultimately new life will come
through

So with more mouths to feed they become this tag
team
One up in the day, then the baton passed at night
No resentment or complaint about their plight.

This goes on for years and as time passes,
A decision is made to seek greener grasses
So a castle is sought, to call their own
They overcome their fear and take out the loan

More time passes and things rumble on
But even with the hiccups the relationship stays
strong
The mouths they have worked hard to maintain and
feed
Grow bigger and older, some develop esteem

Their lot is not as bad as others they know. And they
thank their lucky stars that it is so
However they refuse to rest on their laurels
As what seems easy today, may not be as sweet
tomorrow.

So they continue to labour and toil and are used. By
industries, and agencies shouldering covert abuse.
And with this they balance the struggles of their kin
The babies, the parties and the dramas they get in

They begin to think more strategically
Of a time in the future when only them two, they will
this time build their castle in the island of their birth.
Because isn't this what all the toil and hardship over
the years will have been worth?

Then, just a year before the plan is to be hatched,
and life follows routine, day in and day out. Out of
the blue, the male partner falls ill.

Comes home early from work– not too early of course.
Laid up for the weekend, nothing to write home about

But, by the end of those 48 hours, wailing and bawling
fall in torrents of showers. As he does not make it.

Now, this is where you would think my story would end
But bear with me; if you can, and you will see, it is
true.

That this is only the lead up, to part two…………..

So, crushed and overwhelmed with the loss of her
spouse,
Fearful and unsure of her own clout.
The female cannot, does not, give in.
Head up, shoulders back, she gets stuck in.

She hits the ground running, a true baptism of fire.
Finances, legalities, taxation and more
She works through, deciphers, and when she is sure,
That everything is covered and her husband laid to
rest

She grieves.

She continues to work, as this is all that she knows.
Getting up in the dark, in the wind, in the snow.
Not because she has to. But, because she does not
know how not.

By this time their youngest is just turned 18
Sits quietly watching the developing queen
Knows in her heart that the king is no more
But truly too naïve, to fathom the score.

Cannot truly appreciate the determination and will
of the queen who on target gets on the plane still
And builds that castle, keeps the strategic plan.
Maintains the legacy worked out with her man.

Who sits with her youngest through young loves
distress
And apologises to her that maybe it would have been
best
If she had not waited and had her so late,
So that an elder sibling instead would be there and be
great

But what could be greater, than sharing this pain?
The mother and child, sat side by side crying,
together...........................

More time flashes past and generations expand
Children have grandchildren and grand children great grand's!
And this very same woman is lost in the mire, watching and supporting the results of faddish desire.

And now, as her flesh, begins to weaken
Defying the spirit that is still in its youth
She routinely awakens before 5 every morning
To wash or iron, to still feel of use.

And it is now that the aches and the pains increase steadily
The heads dizzy spells, chest paining more readily
Still she refuses to sit and relax.
Why?
Because there is always another barrel to pack!

So as we draw to the end of this vigorous journey
I hope I have given a clarity divine
Because the women I speak of in all of her glory
Is, naturally, my dear mother of mine

ABOUT THE AUTHOR

Akilah Moseley is a Poet, Writer, Executive Coach and Leadership mentor. When not developing her own creative talents, Akilah's passion involves supporting and enabling those around her to raise their awareness of self and take responsibility in determining their life journey'.

In addition to supporting others to achieve their dreams, Akilah spends her time taking long walks, eating hot food, appreciating the hustle and bustle of family life and striving to always "live, Laugh, Love".

OTHER WORK BY THIS AUTHOR INCLUDED IN:

"Sharing Space" (Inspired Word) 2009
"I-Factor for Women" (New Eyes Press) 2010
A Lime Jewel - Lambi fundraiser for Haiti (Black Londoners) 2010
"Secrets of the Heart" (United press Ltd) 2011
"What is Love?" (United Press Ltd) 2011
Seeds of Inspiration" (United press Ltd) 2011
"Life Begins At..." (United press Ltd) 2011
"In the Minds Eye" (United Press Ltd) 2012
"Pastures New" (United press Ltd) 2012
"Deep Secrets" (United Press Ltd) 2012
"It's A Colourful Life" (United Press Ltd) 2012

LOOK OUT FOR THE NEXT BOOK IN THE SERIES

"Thoughts From a Reasoning Mind - 52 Passages to Sustain a Greater Self" (I. AM.) 2014

www.ingramcontent.com/pod-product-compliance
Lightning Source LLC
Chambersburg PA
CBHW060629030426
42337CB00018B/3262